DEMOS

Demos is an independent think tank committed to radical thinking on the long-term problems facing the UK and other advanced industrial societies.

It aims to develop ideas – both theoretical and practical – to help shape the politics of the twenty first century, and to improve the breadth and depth of political debate.

Demos publishes books and a regular journal and undertakes substantial empirical and policy oriented research projects. Demos is a registered charity.

In all of its work Demos brings together people from a wide range of backgrounds in business, academia, government, the voluntary sector and the media to share and cross-fertilise ideas and experiences.

For further information and
subscription details please contact:
Demos, 9 Bridewell Place, London EC4V 6AP
Tel: 0171 353 4479 Fax: 0171 353 4481
email: mail@demos.co.uk

The employee mutual

Combining flexibility with security in the new world of work

Charles Leadbeater and Stephen Martin

First published in
July 1998

by

Demos
9 Bridewell Place
London EC4V 6AP
Tel: 0171 353 4479
Fax: 0171 353 4481

© Demos/Reed 1998

Arguments 20

ISBN 1 898309 94 9

CONTENTS

Acknowledgements

This Argument follows an earlier Demos report, by Geoff Mulgan and Tom Bentley, upon which we have drawn, which set out the idea of an employee mutual. The proposals in this report were developed through discussions with: Mike Knight, of Speke Community Credit Union; Terry Hunt at the advertising agency Evans Hunt Scott; Stephen Lloyd at solicitors Bates, Wells and Braithwaite; John Edgar of BusinessNet; David Grayson of Business in the Community; Marion Pool of the Association of Friendly Societies; Pat Conaty of the Aston Reinvestment Trust; Elaine Kempson of Bristol University; Jennifer Butterworth at Kingston Citizens Advice Bureau; Helen Evans at Bootstrap Enterprises; and Kate Fokhir at London Borough of Hackney. This research was made possible by a generous grant from Reed, the recruitment specialists, and publication was kindly sponsored by St Luke's, the advertising agency.

Foreword

Mutual aid is still the kernel of society. Unless we helped each other in all manner of ways, we should be quickly back to the jungle. The Victorians saw this. Prince Kropotkin saw this in his great book on mutual aid. A greater figure than him, the Scottish philosopher-king, David Hume, saw it in his book on ethics. Fellow feeling, he said again and again, is the axiom of society. Mutual aid is fellow feeling expressed not from the pulpit or the despatch box, but in action.

Every age (for individuals as they grow older and for societies as they change across the face of history) has its own way of putting the principle into practice. The sad thing about our present century has been that mutual aid has been the general keynote only in war and the immediate aftermath of war, when the solidarity of war is carried into peace. The problem of peace has been to find a moral substitute for war, and in a society that has become ever more affluent (but not for the poor) we have not done too well in the search. We need new forms in which the elemental need can be satisfied, and we have been short of them. I have done a little. I set up the Consumers' Association for mutual aid. Millions of people have pooled their subscriptions to finance a common, non-profit service – of testing goods and services and passing on the results to each other – which has helped to improve the quality of what consumers get.

I started the College of Health to do something similar for patients and to give some support to the self-help groups in health – 3,000 of them by now. Our magazine was called *Self-Health* and then *Health Which*. It was the same with the University of the Third Age, which is a means whereby older people can teach others without money passing. It has flourished. There are now hundreds of these universities across the length and breadth of this land. It is similar to the Brain Train, where commuters teach one another on the journey.

But these are no more than a few examples. Before the moral tone of society can be changed, much more is needed. We need new forms for old ideals.

This is why I welcome this new idea from the ever-creative Demos. I regard it as one of the spiritual descendants of Hume. Hail to a new idea: the Employee Mutual.

Michael Young

Summary

The employee mutual

● The employee mutual would be a new organisation in the labour market. It would help people to find work, improve their skills and manage their working lives. It would help employers to fill vacancies and bring together workers and businesses to meet shared needs for training and childcare.

● The employee mutual would be designed to operate in the modern flexible labour market. People's working lives are becoming an increasingly diverse mix of full-time and part-time work, permanent and temporary jobs, self-employment, lifelong learning, parenting and joblessness. Relationships between employers and employees are increasingly transitory. The pace of this change means people will have to take more responsibility for the management of their careers. The employee mutual would offer them a stable relationship and support. It would provide a degree of security without restricting the dynamism which flexible labour markets bring.

● Membership of the employee mutual would be particularly valuable for those at the lower end of the labour market, which is characterised by insecure work on the one hand and the rigidities of the benefit system on the other. The mutual would help members to spring the benefit trap and offer them some stability once in work.

● The employee mutual would benefit businesses as well as individuals, helping firms to meet their staffing requirements and delivering essential services. In particular, it would help small businesses to develop cost-effective solutions to common needs, such as training. The structure of the mutual would recognise the interdependence of employees and employers.

A membership organisation

● The employee mutual would be a membership organisation, a form of club. It would be owned and controlled by its members, and have a democratic, participative structure. It would be a local institution, highly responsive to the needs of its members, who would have a clear stake in their mutual and in the services it would deliver.

- Jobless individuals, employees, the self-employed and small and large businesses would all be members of the employee mutual. This diverse membership would give the mutual extensive contacts and resources. By bringing employed and unemployed members together, it would reconnect the jobless with the world of work, rather than isolating them in their own 'schemes'. Some employee mutuals would be open to all individuals in a locality. Others would cater for specific groups, such as lone parents, or members of an ethnic or religious community.

- Membership would be voluntary, and members would make a clear commitment to the cooperative aims of the employee mutual. That commitment would be enshrined in a covenant, which all members would sign, that would set out the contributions they would make to the mutual. The mutual's cooperative ethos would impose an internal discipline which recognised that rights go with responsibilities. For the jobless, membership would be a form of accreditation, providing prospective employers with evidence of their commitment to work.

- The mutual would be run by a small full-time management team. The team's main task would be to organise the members to provide one another with self-help. A job-search coordinator would help to train and organise job 'hit squads' which would scour the locality for work on behalf of mutual members. A childcare coordinator would bring members together to run a nursery and crèche facilities and to provide childcare at home. Members would be trained to act as mentors, helping fellow members to make benefit claims, get into work and manage their personal finances.

Inputs and outputs

- Employees and self-employed members of the employee mutual would pay a weekly membership fee of perhaps £3 to £5 per week. Jobless members would make a token contribution of 50p per week, but would contribute at least fifteen hours per week of services in kind, helping with childcare, job search, benefits advice, marketing, administration and maintenance. Employed members could contribute services in kind such as mentoring.

- Employer members would make regular financial contributions. In addition, they would commit to register their vacancies with the employee mutual and to interview any member referred to them. Large employers would provide additional services in kind, such as business advice, secondees, access to in-house training courses and use of equipment and premises.

- In return for these contributions, members would be entitled to use the work-related services provided by the employee mutual, such as training courses, job search and childcare. By putting something into the mutual, members would get a clear entitlement to take something out. Members would earn points on a smartcard which would enable them to 'buy' services from the mutual.

- Employers and working members would, where appropriate, pay charges for services. The cost would be reduced by the services in kind being provided by mutual members. Also, the employee mutual would encourage employers and individuals to find innovative ways of sharing the costs and risks of delivering services. For example, a mutual might work with a large employer to set up a nursery or an open learning facility which would be used by both organisations. The mutual would also apply for public funds to finance training programmes.

- Special benefit rules would apply to members of the employee mutual. These rules would make it easier for members to combine income from part-time or temporary work with benefits and ensure that they receive benefits promptly. This would greatly reduce the insecurity which deters people from making the transition from welfare to work. The internal discipline of the mutual would prevent members from 'taking advantage' of the modified benefit rules.

- For employers, the employee mutual would act as an employment agency, providing full-time, part-time, permanent and temporary staff. It would offer employers quality assurance, money-back and replacement guarantees, and cover for absences, all of which would reduce the risk to the employer of taking on a member of the mutual. For individual members, the mutual would play a brokering role, enabling them to combine two part-time jobs, or to combine a part-time job with training, or to take study leave by providing someone to cover for them.

- Small businesses find it particularly difficult to provide their employees with training and childcare. The employee mutual would help them to do so in a cost-effective fashion. Self-employed members would be provided with business services, such as the use of IT facilities, and the mutual would encourage the formation of support networks for the self-employed.

- The employee mutual's core tasks would be work-related. But a mature mutual could take on a wider role: providing members with financial services through a credit union; helping small businesses to devise development plans; working in partnership with the local authority to promote economic development; organising consumer discounts for members.

- A distinctive feature of the employee mutual is that the same institution would give people support throughout the labour market 'life-cycle'. The mutual would provide an unemployed person with preparation to re-enter employment, such as basic skills training, and help the person to find work. If necessary, the mutual would arrange for childcare. If the person lost their job, they would turn to the mutual for advice on reapplying for benefits, as well as for social contact and emotional support. If the job lasted, the mutual would continue to deliver childcare and offer opportunities to upskill. The employee mutual would provide a durable relationship amid the constant change of the flexible labour market.

Creating the employee mutual

- A sustainable employee mutual would take three years to develop and require a membership of at least 2,000. During the start-up phase, an employee mutual would require public funding and other sponsorship, but within three to five years most of its operations should be self-financing. Some mutuals could grow out of existing self-help community organisations.

- For the employee mutual to thrive, the support of central government would be crucial. In particular, government would need to modify the benefit rules applying to mutual members, create tax incentives for individuals and businesses to participate, and establish a legal and regulatory framework headed by a national council for employee mutuals.

- A series of pilots would test how the employee mutual model would work in different labour markets and with different memberships. If the pilots proved successful, the aim should be to create a national movement of at least 250 employee mutuals with at least half a million members by 2007. If the top 250 FTSE companies each sponsored one 'social entrepreneur' charged with launching a mutual, the achievement of this goal would be brought much closer.

- The employee mutual would be a new institution designed to work with the grain of the flexible labour market and would be the first major investment in social infrastructure for decades. By bringing employers and workers together in an ethic of cooperative self-improvement, it would marry flexibility with security on modern terms.

1. Introduction

Modern market economies such as Britain's are searching for a way to marry flexibility with security. That search is at the heart of modern politics, particularly in approaches to employment and welfare policy. As a society we need to match the attractions of individualism and choice, the dynamism of the market and competition, with measures to promote cohesion, mutual self-help and belonging.

Spurred by political, economic and cultural changes, society has become both more privatised and individualised in the past two decades. People are more likely to seek private solutions to problems than public ones; they are more likely to measure their satisfaction and well-being in individual rather than collective terms. The ethic of the times is one of autonomy, self-governance and choice.

The growth of individualism troubles some people who extol the virtues of more settled communities or the merits of old-style public sector institutions to regulate change. That is not the position taken by this report. It would be a mistake to address modern social and economic problems by reimposing old public sector solutions. The appeal of nostalgic notions of community is not shared by many young people and would turn out to be illusory. Instead, this report seeks an innovative solution to a modern set of problems: its aim is to develop contemporary institutions, designed to address the problems created by the contemporary labour market.

Open market societies such as Britain face a problem of balance: the extension of private choice and individualism has not been matched by investments in social institutions able to draw together a more diverse society and offer its members a degree of security in the face of change. Nowhere is that search for a modern way to match flexibility with security more pressing than in the labour market.

The British labour market has become far more flexible in the past two decades. Flexibility is a term used to cover several interrelated trends: the shift from manufacturing to service jobs and from large to small employers; the abolition of many demarcation lines at work and the rise of multi-skilling; the introduction of more flexible pay systems; the rise of self-employment, part-time and temporary jobs and the decline of traditional, full-time, permanent jobs in large organisations; the prevalence of much more variable hours of work; and perhaps most dramatically, increased participation by women in the workforce, resulting in a far greater number of people combining work and parenting. All of these developments are ways in which the labour market has become more fluid and forms of employment have become more diverse.

Flexible labour markets are more dynamic, respond to change more quickly and thus are better able to create jobs than more regulated labour markets. With technological change accelerating and more of the economy open to international competition, there is a strong case for labour markets that encourage people to switch from occupations and industries in decline to those that are expanding. For many individuals, especially those with skills, the flexible labour market offers the stimulation of new opportunities and continuous learning.

New forms of flexibility have brought new costs, however. There are the personal, and often psychological, costs of the growing insecurity and anxiety created by more unstable and diverse patterns of employment. Many people are changing jobs more frequently and therefore face significant changes to how they are paid, their hours of work and their tasks. Work is a vital source of status and identity for people. Upheavals in the nature of work and careers mean more change in people's sense of themselves. In addition to accelerating change, people are increasingly having to rely on their own resources to cope with the uncertainties created by that change, and to manage their careers and skills development. Some commentators argue that flexible labour markets also create social costs, in the form of declining trust and social cohesion.

The flexible labour market has imposed the highest costs, however, on those on its lowest rungs. For the low skilled and low paid, the labour market has in important respects become more rigid in the past two decades. The growth of long-term unemployment, concentrated among workless households, is one such rigidity. For the unemployed, the labour market has become less accessible: it has become more difficult for someone to move out of unemployment into work than it was in the 1970s. Income mobility among the low paid has declined: fewer poor people are working their way up to higher wages than used to. And wage inequality has risen markedly. Falling demand for unskilled labour, combined with an out-dated benefit system, has resulted in a labour market which is more stratified, less fluid and less secure for many poorly skilled people.

One important source of these costs is the institutions that are meant to regulate or underpin the labour market by providing training or by helping employees and employers to share risks. Many of these institutions were designed for an industrial world of male full-employment that has gone for good. The role of large employers, trade unions and tripartite institutions has declined markedly in the last two decades, partly as a result of the policies of the Conservative governments, but mainly because the economic base has shifted away from them.

Large companies, which were once a mechanism through which workers and employers shared the risks of adjusting to change, have adopted a much more aggressive approach to labour costs since the early 1980s. They also employ a smaller proportion of the workforce than two decades ago.

Trade unions are largely creatures of the manufacturing and public sectors. They are poorly represented in the fastest growing areas of the flexible labour market, among small companies and in the service sector, among young workers and women. Much of the British workforce now works in a fluid labour market, beyond the reach of large organisations, whether those be companies, the public sector or trade unions (though the lives of benefit claimants are still closely bound up with large bureaucracies). As a consequence, not only do many workers lack a collective voice, more importantly they do not have easy access to institutions capable of providing the support needed to thrive in a modern labour market: job search, training, childcare.

Any attempt to address the insecurity that flexible labour markets bring in their wake needs to work with the grain of flexibility, not against it. One option would be to implement market-based solutions, such as private insurance schemes to protect people against risks. A second would be to reform traditional risk pooling institutions, such as trade unions, so that they can play a more constructive role within the emerging service economy. Each of these approaches has merits but also limitations. This report makes a case for an innovative response: to create a modern mutual institution – an employee mutual – through which people and businesses can provide one another with help and security within a flexible labour market.

The employee mutual is an attempt to marry flexibility with security on modern terms. The employee mutual would be a local membership organisation with a small full-time staff. Its members would mainly be the unemployed, the employed, the self-employed and owner-managers running small businesses. Large businesses and voluntary organisations could also join a mutual in their locality. Members would sign a covenant committing them to help one another to find work and to develop their skills, careers and businesses. Members would contribute to the mutual by paying a membership fee, if they could afford to do so, or by contributing services in kind. In addition the employee mutual would be eligible for public funds, for instance from the Single Regeneration Budget.

The employee mutual would use these financial and human resources to provide its members with a range of services, which would help them to chart their way through the turbulence of the modern labour market. These services would include childcare, job search, training, benefits advice and business services for the self-employed. The unemployed members of an employee mutual would be given special benefits guarantees which would allow them to move into work more easily. Small businesses would turn to the employee mutual for help in filling vacancies and developing their enterprises. A successful, mature employee mutual could also provide its members with a range of financial services. The employee mutual would be a source of cooperative self-help, especially valuable to those in insecure employment or seeking to move from welfare to work.

Each era of economic development has created institutions which have brought people together to share risks. Industrialisation created trade unions and friendly societies. The middle of the twentieth century was dominated by the emergence of large, often overly bureaucratic, organisations: general trade unions, large corporations and the welfare state. We are now experiencing the creation of a far more flexible labour market, driven by technological and cultural change, in which services and small businesses will be the predominant sources of employment. This new economy will require more resilience, self-reliance and entrepreneurship on the part of individuals. It will also require risk-sharing institutions which are smaller, more adaptable and more responsive to their members' needs, and which do not create rigidities themselves. We need to create distinctive modern labour market institutions which help people to prosper from flexibility rather than be overwhelmed by it.

The case for the employee mutual stems from its capacity to resolve the problems that flexible labour markets create, without undermining the benefits that flexibility brings. This capacity to marry flexibility with security makes the employee mutual better suited to the modern labour market than other institutions, which were created by and for an old industrial economy which is now being transformed.

2. The flexible labour market and the employee mutual

The shift from manufacturing to services, deregulation and de-unionisation, the application of new workplace technologies, outsourcing and other changes to the structure of the modern company, and the continued rise in women's participation in work, have all contributed to the increase in labour market flexibility. In future, working lives will become an increasingly diverse mix of jobs (permanent and temporary, full-time and part-time) and other activities, education and training, parenting and unemployment. The employee mutual would help members to cope with the stresses created by this diversity, while enabling them to take advantage of the opportunities a flexible labour market can bring. The pressures and needs created by the flexible labour market, which the employee mutual would attempt to respond to, are set out in Figure 1 overleaf.

2.1 Change and insecurity

There is a widespread sense that jobs have become more insecure. For men at least it is true that jobs do not last as long as they used to. Average job tenure is at an all-time low for men. In 1975, median length of job tenure for men was eight years and two months. By 1995 that had fallen to six years and six months, and it has continued to fall since. Job tenure for women (except those aged under 25) has risen significantly over the last two decades, but this is probably due mainly to increased use of maternity leave. Paul Gregg and Jonathan Wadsworth, from the London School of Economics, have argued that the insecurity which people say they feel may result from the greater likelihood that a job will end, combined with a sharp increase in the costs associated with unemployment (see 2.4 below).

One aspect of this sense of insecurity is that redundancies seem to have become a permanent feature of the labour market. An Institute of Personnel and Development survey of labour turnover in 1996 found that over 60 per cent of organisations had used vol-

Figure 1. The pressures of a flexible labour market

Development	Need
Permanent jobs of short duration	Help people through career changes
Growth in part-time and temporary work	Package part-time and temporary jobs together, or combine with other activities 'Flexible' benefit system
Rise in women's employment	Childcare 'Family-friendly' working patterns
Growth in self-employment	Support networks and business services for home-based workers
Growth of micro-businesses	Training, childcare, recruitment services
Long-term unemployment and rise in economic inactivity	Keep unemployed in contact with work Job preparation and systematic job search
Workless households	Help to spring benefit traps
Cycling between unemployment and insecure, low paid jobs	Support people through transitions from work to benefits and back again Upskilling

untary or compulsory redundancies during that year, despite the economic recovery and the tightness of the labour market. Redundancy programmes are being driven by the search for cost savings, the introduction of new technology and internal reorganisation. Even when the economy is growing strongly, the pressures of competition and technological change mean that employers keep a close watch on labour costs. The intensification of these pressures has resulted in a significant change in management outlook over the past decade or so. Large employers are reluctant to share with their employees the risks inherent in rapid change. Employees are under increasing pressure to justify their pay through performance, to work longer hours and to provide for their own security.

The widely reported sense that work is less secure and more demanding than it used to be is one consequence of these changes. Individuals are increasingly required to take responsibility for their own career development. Yet the accelerating pace of change means that their need for support, such as careers advice, help to identify new job opportunities and help to access education and training, is increasing. The employee mutual will help to fill that gap. Relationships between employers and employees are becoming more transitory. In this context, people will value the long-term relationships and sense of belonging that the employee mutual will provide.

2.2 Part-time and temporary work
One of the most important ingredients in the creation of Britain's more flexible labour market has been the rise of part-time work. Part-timers account for about a quarter of the workforce, up from a fifth in 1980. The growth in part-time employment dates back to the 1950s and is closely linked to the rise in female participation in the labour market. In 1996, women made up a third of the full-time workforce but 82 per cent of those working part-time; 44 per cent of women in employment worked part-time, compared with 8 per cent of men. The rise in part-time work has been substantially driven by the demand from women for work roles which can be combined with parenting (albeit in the absence of substantial state support for childcare). According to the Labour Force Survey, only one in ten women part-timers took a part-time job because they could not find full-time work, although the figure is higher for men at one in four. Of course, the growth in part-time employment is not entirely supply driven: many employers use part-time workers as a way of matching labour supply better to consumer demand.

Largely as a result of the growth in part-time work, and of the pressure towards longer hours for full-time workers, less than 10 per cent of employees work a 'standard' 40-hour week. In 1979, almost half the workforce worked between 33 and 44 hours a week. In 1996, only a third did, with a third working much longer hours and the other third markedly shorter hours. At the beginning of that year, about 565,000 people reported that their usual weekly hours of work were five or less.

Over the past decade and a half, the use of temporary contracts has grown even faster than part-time work. Temporary employment rose from about 5 per cent of those in employment in 1984 to 7.1 per cent in 1996, although most of this rise occurred during the 1990s recovery and the extent to which it is a cyclical phenomenon is unclear.

Within this growth, the character of temporary work has changed. The proportion of temporary workers undertaking casual or seasonal work (heavily represented in sectors such as construction and tourism) has declined in recent years in favour of those on fixed-term contracts and temporaries supplied by recruitment agencies. Fixed-term contracts make up about a half of temporary jobs. Temporary jobs are lasting longer: in 1996, about 40 per cent of such jobs lasted more than a year. Employers continue to use temporary workers for 'traditional' reasons, such as cover for absent employees. The growth in temporary work, however, and changes to its character have been driven by organisations seeking to match the supply of labour as closely as possible to demand. Although temporary jobs make up a relatively small share of total employment, they account for about one in three new engagements, in part because they are increasingly used by employers as a trial period prior to granting a permanent contract.

The rise in part-time work, 'atypical' hours and various forms of temporary employment is creating an increasingly diverse labour market. The employee mutual would enable its members to navigate their way through the flexible labour market, helping people to move from job to job. The employee mutual would be a jobs broker, helping to match employers' demand for flexibility to workers' demand for a degree of stability. Employment agencies have been brokering temporary jobs in this way for decades.

The employee mutual would perform a similar role, helping its members to move through a series of temporary jobs into permanent employment if they desired. The mutual could help members to combine two part-time jobs, or to combine part-time work with training. By providing a member to cover in their absence, it could enable an employed member to take a sabbatical or extended parental leave.

2.3 The self-employed and small firms

It is not just employees and the unemployed that need help. The self-employed and micro-businesses often lack support services and either have to buy them on the market or call in favours from friends. The share of employment accounted for by self-employment and small firms has increased significantly over the past two decades. Self-employment grew from 1.9 million in 1979 to 3.3 million in 1997. Micro-businesses employing no more than a handful of people have also grown rapidly. There were 3.7 million enterprises in the UK at the start of 1996, an increase of 1.3 million since 1980, according to the Department of Trade and Industry. Of these, 2.5 million had no employees, 1.2 million had between one and 49 employees and only 32,000 had 50 or more. Micro-enterprises employing less than five people accounted in 1994 for 89 per cent of all enterprises and a quarter of all employment, according to a report published by the Employment Policy Institute in 1996.

Small businesses operate in a volatile world, and their employees share in this insecurity. During the 1980s one in ten businesses left the VAT register in any one year. Small firms provide less training than larger firms, offer fewer employee benefits and tend to pay lower wages, sometimes cash-in-hand. In a fast-moving and competitive economy, small firms have some natural advantages and can enjoy spectacular growth. The UK economy also has a large number of financially insecure small firms, however, which compete on cost rather than quality or innovation. One of the roles of the employee mutual would be to offer training services for the employees of small businesses and to help their employers to translate new skills into improved business performance.

Small businesses need support as much as the workers who work for them; the two are inextricably linked. An employee mutual would seek to make life more secure for employees, in part by providing their micro-employers with cost-effective services and support. Apart from training, services would include recruitment (including short-term help during a crisis) and childcare. Local employers would be members of the mutual, and close links between the individual members and employer members would help to make the mutual's services more effective for both parties.

2.4 The unemployed

As well as providing those in flexible employment with greater security, the mutual must also address the needs of the unemployed, who face a labour market that has become more stratified. Unemployment has become self-reinforcing for many people. It has become harder for an unemployed person to move into employment and more likely that someone unemployed will become economically inactive or work in the cash-in-hand economy. The longer people remain unemployed, the harder it becomes for them to maintain contact with the jobs market. This would be one of the employee mutual's main tasks: to keep the unemployed in contact with the world of work and provide them with a route back into employment.

The costs of becoming unemployed are much greater than they used to be, partly because the value of benefits has fallen relative to earnings. More importantly, demand for low-skilled labour has fallen as a result of technological change and globalisation. This has led to a pronounced fall in the relative earnings of the low-skilled and a decline in their job security. These trends have created formidable barriers to work. The longer a person is out of work, or the more incidents of unemployment they experience, the more the disadvantage of unemployment compounds itself.

According to Gregg and Wadsworth's work, the chances of

someone moving from unemployment into employment during the course of a year fell from 47 per cent in 1977 to 36 per cent in 1995. In contrast, the chances of someone who was unemployed becoming inactive rose from 8 per cent to 20 per cent. Typically, people now spend 20 per cent longer in unemployment than they did in the 1970s.

For those who succeed in finding a job after a spell of unemployment, it is likely that the new job will compare poorly with the one that was lost. Jobs taken by unemployed people tend to pay less than average and are more likely to be part time or casual; in 1994, 'entry jobs' taken by the unemployed paid only 44 per cent of gross weekly wages of all other jobs (providing on average 25 per cent fewer hours work at 65 per cent of average hourly pay). The risk of returning to unemployment is high. According to a report on those leaving unemployment published by the Treasury this year, a quarter are back on the register within three months and half return within a year. This reflects the unstable nature of many jobs at the lower end of the labour market, as well as the personal difficulties which make it hard for some people to stay in work. Moreover, the fall in the relative earnings of the low skilled has been accompanied by a decline in their wage mobility. According to analysis conducted by the Employment Policy Institute, of those wage earners in the bottom 10 per cent of the wage distribution in 1989, only 31 per cent of men and 29 per cent of women had managed to improve their position five years later. This means that alongside the long-term unemployed and inactive, there is another group who are trapped in a cycle of recurring unemployment and unstable poorly paid jobs.

The falling value of pay in entry jobs is one of two main reasons for the reduced likelihood of leaving unemployment. The other is a benefit system designed for a world of male full employment in which wages were stable and significantly higher than benefits. These days the wages of a job taken by someone who has just left unemployment are far less likely to pay them a clear margin above benefits. This disincentive is particularly powerful for individuals with unemployed spouses, a fact which has contributed to the rise in the proportion of 'workless' households. The benefit system creates significant financial disincentives for people to take work (the 'unemployment trap') and to increase earnings when on in-work benefits (the 'poverty trap').

These traps, though important, are not the whole story. A survey conducted by the Joseph Rowntree Foundation in 1996 found that just under half of benefit claimants based their decision to take or refuse a job on an economic calculation of whether their income would be greater in employment. For many others, the desire to work was overriding. But the benefit system creates disincentives to work in another crucial way: the insecurity of the transition from unemployment benefits to in-work benefits and from work back to unemployment benefits should a job not last.

Job seekers often do not understand which in-work benefits they are entitled to. They doubt whether they will be paid promptly. Returning to unemployment benefits after a period in employment can be a frustrating, drawn out process. An interruption in the payment of benefits, either when moving from welfare to work or back again, can have disastrous consequences for a poor household. One of the main obstacles discouraging people from moving from welfare into work is the fear that the job will not last, a fear which reflects the casual nature of many entry jobs. For many people, income on benefits is at least predictable; in contrast the jobs market seems perilously unstable. One of the employee mutual's roles would be to provide security during this transition between welfare and work. Another would be to make benefit rules easier to understand for its members. A third would be to provide a framework within which the recently unemployed could improve their skills and earnings potential, rather than getting trapped at the bottom of the labour market.

The self-reinforcing nature of joblessness stems, to some extent, from employers' perception of the unemployed. Employers place great importance on qualities such as a positive attitude, commitment to the job, work disciplines (such as punctuality and the ability to work without close supervision) and interpersonal skills. The longer someone is unemployed, the more difficult it becomes for them to satisfy an employer that they have the requisite motivation and work discipline, partly because many jobless people are isolated and partly because they often lack the confidence and communication skills to do well in an interview. Membership of the employee mutual would help to keep the unemployed in contact with the world of work and provide direct evidence of commitment. The employee mutual would make it less risky for employers to recruit unemployed people.

The non-employed are not a homogeneous group. As the employee mutual would be close to its members, its services could be tailored to their needs. Lone mothers, for example, face particular problems getting jobs. The majority of lone mothers want to work; it is not a lack of motivation that holds them back. The limited availability, and relatively high cost, of childcare is one obstacle, but so too is a lack of qualifications, which results in low earnings potential. The disruption of moving off benefit into a low paid job, and the complexity and delays involved in renegotiating the benefit system if the job is soon lost, are particularly strong disincentives when a fragile family budget is at stake. As a result, many lone mothers, especially those with poor qualifications, are much more likely to develop strategies to cope on benefits. An employee mutual for lone parents, based around a nursery, could address all of these problems, helping to provide childcare, training, job search and benefits advice. This is just one example of how an employee mutual could be tailored to the needs of a specific group. Another might be a mutual for disabled workers or a mutual for the long-term unemployed in a former industrial centre.

2.5 Family-friendly policies and equal opportunities

Difficulty in gaining access to quality childcare is a major barrier to work for many parents. The supply of childcare is inadequate and parents lack the financial assistance they need. According to the Daycare Trust, in 1995 there were nearly 6 million children under the age of eight in Britain but less than 700,000 registered childcare places. Childcare fees in Britain are among the highest in Europe. Establishing a nursery as a business is a precarious exercise; a Daycare Trust survey conducted in 1991 found that of 34 attempts to set up a private nursery, only fourteen were successful, and a majority of the 'successful' entrepreneurs did not consider that they were getting a return on their investment. The employee mutual would share the risks and costs of establishing and maintaining childcare facilities among members (who would contribute their time to run the nursery as well as cash), employers and the state.

Research undertaken for the Department for Education and Employment shows that smaller businesses are less likely to offer their employees assistance with childcare, or to offer other family-friendly policies such as extra-statutory maternity benefits and flexible work patterns to accommodate childcare needs. The employee mutual would help to broker work patterns which suited both individual members and employers, for example by finding members to cover for a term-time worker during the school holidays.

In providing a job placement service, the employee mutual would act as a local advocate for its individual members, in particular those facing some form of discrimination. This would be backed up by advice to employers, for example on how to make adjustments under the Disability Discrimination Act. One effect would be to maximise the local supply of labour available to employers.

Conclusion
The labour market has become more fluid and more flexible, with the growth of self-employment, part-time and temporary work. Permanent jobs are likely to last less long. More jobs are being created by very small businesses lacking even basic human resource policies. People need to be resilient to prosper in the modern labour market. Many would benefit from joining an institution which would pool risks and reduce the uncertainties they face, without restricting their opportunities, and without undermining the dynamism that flexible labour markets bring. The

employee mutual's role would be to help the unemployed and employed, the self-employed and small businesses to cope better with this fluidity. It would work not just for workers, but for their employers as well, to find better solutions to shared problems of job search, recruitment, training and child care. The employee mutual would be designed to operate at the very heart of the flexible labour market, permitting, and indeed facilitating flexible working. It would offer security and support by going with the grain of flexibility.

3. The employee mutual model

The blueprint for an employee mutual set out in this section is deliberately general. Many kinds of employee mutual (EM) could be established to meet the needs of different local labour markets and different memberships.

3.1 Features of the EM model

The key features of a model employee mutual, which would apply to all EMs, are as follows:

- the employee mutual would be a membership organisation
- members would sign a covenant with other members
- the mutual's primary function would be to provide work-related services
- services would be financed by membership fees, charges to users, and other sources of funding
- members would also provide one another with services in kind
- a simple points system would allow members to claim services from the mutual by making contributions to it
- these points would be stored on an employee mutual smart-card
- the mutual would be a local, responsive institution.

A membership organisation

An EM would be like a club. It would be a self-help organisation with members from among the unemployed and the employed, the self-employed and small businesses, as well as large companies and voluntary organisations. Membership would be voluntary and the act of joining would involve a clear commitment: it could not be undertaken lightly. The EM would be controlled by its members and would have an open, democratic, participative style. But the EM would not be a cooperative; it would be a company limited by guarantee, with a small full-time management team.

Individual membership could vary between EMs. Some EMs would be open to all workers within a catchment area; others might be set up for specific groups, such as lone parents or a religious community, and tailor their services to those groups. An EM could not be for the unemployed alone, as this would defeat its purpose of bringing the unemployed into contact with the employed in the search for work. The EM is not a scheme for the jobless.

The mixed nature of the membership – embracing the unemployed and employed, employers and voluntary organisations – would provide the EM with a wide range of resources, information and contacts. By mixing workers and employers, it would ensure its services were relevant to both sides of the employment relationship.

How members would join
Joining an EM would involve more than signing on occasionally. The unemployed would not be referred to the EM by the Employment Service, although it could be one of the options highlighted at the Job Centre. An unemployed applicant would have to choose to join the EM, and would go through an interview and an orientation day so that both mutual and applicant could assess whether it would be the right option for them. All members would have to sign a membership covenant, which would pledge them to help other members and make regular membership contributions, either financially or through services in kind. Membership fees would vary depending on the status of the members: whether they were working or unemployed, a small or large business.

For each member, the covenant would contain a series of pledges. These would vary according to the status of the member, whether unemployed, employed, self-employed or an employer. For example, an unemployed member might pledge to: accept a probationary period of three months in which eligibility to membership could be assessed; make scheduled membership contributions in cash and in kind; actively look for work opportunities, both for themselves and on behalf of the EM as a whole; accept any work opportunities offered which met pre-agreed criteria;

undertake training; help other members to get into work by sharing information and offering advice; and remain a member of the mutual even after they got a job, sticking with it to help subsequent members. The covenant signed by an employer would set down their commitments to the EM, for example to notify all vacancies to the mutual, to guarantee an interview to anyone referred by the mutual and to provide mentoring for unemployed members.

Providing work-related services to individuals and firms

The EM would use the resources put in by its members, and other sources of funding, to provide its members with services that would give them greater security, especially at the fragmented lower end of the labour market. The EM would offer a range of work-related services to individuals and firms, such as training and job search. An important feature of these services would be their continuity; for members, the EM could always be relied upon regardless of changes to their employment status or business fortunes.

The EM's core task would be to open a new route into employment by bringing together jobseekers and employers, offering a job search service to the former and a recruitment service to the latter. The EM would also offer a wide range of related services, such as childcare and career guidance. These would be offered to employers as well as employees and the unemployed. The services provided by the EM are discussed in detail in 3.2 below.

A clear basis for exchange

The EM would not be a charity. The mutual would have a cooperative ethic, but it would only succeed by harnessing the self-interest of its members as well. All members would want to be sure that they earned a good return on the resources they put into the mutual. Members would have to receive clear, fair, predictable rewards for whatever mix of resources and effort they put into the club. All members would have a 'price list' of services, which would set out what services they would get access to, in exchange for what level of input. Effort and reward would need to be clearly linked to avoid the mutual principle breaking down.

One possibility would be for the EM to have its own 'club currency', akin to points on the Tesco Club Card. As a member paid into the club, through financial contributions, time and services in kind, they would earn points on their card, which they could spend on services such as childcare and training. As with the Tesco Club Card, the member would get a quarterly statement of the credit on their account. This would give members a tangible sense of what their efforts were buying, in a currency they could cash in.

A simpler approach would be to link contributions to services on a sliding scale. For example, a lone mother might apply to join the mutual and ask to be paid in childcare. Her contract with the mutual would stipulate how many hours work she would have to put in marketing the services of the mutual to local businesses to earn her childcare credits. An unemployed single young man might want to be paid in training to earn qualifications. His contract with the mutual would require him to search for jobs for a set number of hours each week, on behalf of mutual members, to get access to a training course. Jobs within the EM, from acting as a treasurer to staffing the cafeteria, would attract credits which could be spent on services. A willingness to take on obligations to others would be rewarded by access to services.

A local responsive institution

The EM would be a local institution, tailored to local needs. It would not be part of the public sector but it would deliver public sector training, education and unemployment programmes. Its relatively small size and self-governance would allow it to adapt its services and strategies to local economic conditions, vary them across the business cycle and innovate by drawing on the diverse experience of its mixed membership.

An EM would need a small professional staff to provide expertise in administration, financial management and fundraising, and would need to train members to provide the EM's services. Although the EM would aim to generate as many work opportunities as possible for its members inside the organisation, it would also need to recruit from outside qualified individuals such as childcarers and trainers, at least to begin with. A careful balance would have to be struck between professionalism and the mutual's self-help ethos. By striking that balance, the EM would remain responsive to its members. It would minimise the red tape and distrust which characterise the delivery of public employment, training and welfare services by giving members a say in how they should be organised.

3.2 What members would put into an EM

Members would earn their entitlement to services by making contributions to the mutual in a variety of financial and non-financial forms. The kinds of contributions that might be made by an illustrative list of members are set out in Figure 2 opposite.

Employees and the self-employed
People who could afford to do so would pay a membership fee of perhaps £3 to £5 a week to the mutual. They would also pay for services, such as training and childcare, although these would be cheaper than elsewhere. They could make contributions in kind, by providing their time as mentors or by providing job search leads. Self-employed people could be charged by the EM for services such as office support and the use of IT facilities.

The unemployed
The unemployed would not be able to make more than a token financial contribution of perhaps 50p per week to the mutual. They would make up their contribution in the form of at least fifteen hours voluntary work providing services in kind. For instance, the EM could train unemployed members to provide childcare for those in work. An EM which ran its own nursery could train some members as fully qualified carers who would work full time; other members would provide additional care on a part-time basis under the supervision of their qualified colleagues. Unemployed members could work in job search teams.

By canvassing local employers on the telephone and in person, they would identify a pool of job opportunities for other members as well as themselves. These teams would act as the mutual's sales force, marketing its services and encouraging employers to join. Unemployed people could become trainers in basic skills, such as literacy, and act as mentors for their peers, an approach

Figure 2. What members would put into an employee mutual

Member	Financial contribution	Non-financial contribution
Employee	Membership fee Charges for EM services	Mentoring Job openings References
Self-employed	Membership fee Charges for EM services	Mentoring
Unemployed	Token	Services in kind: help with childcare, marketing, job-search hit squads, EM administration etc.
Large business	Membership fee Charges for EM services, eg recruitment, training, childcare Start-up sponsorship Collateral for loans	Commit to register vacancies with EM Secondees Mentors Equipment Business advice
Small business	Membership fee Charges for EM services	Commit to register vacancies with EM
Local authority	Use EM as channel for economic development programmes	Local support and contacts
Central government	Public funding, SRB, New Deal, etc	
Voluntary sector	Membership fee	Placements on voluntary work programmes

which has been successfully adopted by Bootstrap Enterprises in Hackney, east London. A small number of opportunities would be created in the administration of the mutual and the maintenance of its facilities. By providing services in kind, unemployed members would gain an entitlement to other services.

Business membership

Companies would pay a fee to join the mutual, depending on the size and turnover of the business. Fees might range from £20 per week for large businesses to as little as £5 per week for small firms. More importantly, businesses would be customers of the mutual, buying from it services such as job placement, training and childcare. Employers who joined the mutual would benefit from lower fees for these services. They would also be partners in its development, helping to shape its policies and practices. Employers would help to validate the EM's training programmes and legitimise its activities in the eyes of other employers. Very large companies might help by sponsoring their local mutual, providing it with office space and staff secondees. Companies could work with an EM to pool the cost of services in which they had a mutual interest, for example by sharing a nursery or an open-learning facility.

Public sector partners

The public sector would contribute to the mutual in several ways. The most important contribution from central government would be the modifications to the benefit rules discussed in Part 4, which would help EM members move between benefits and employment. The EM would also be able to apply for funds for training and employment programmes, including TEC funds, the Single Regeneration Budget and EU funds, and would require public funding to help cover its launch costs. At a local level, councils could become sponsors of the mutual, contributing premises, staff or financial assistance. A well-developed EM could also become a channel for local authority service delivery, such as council support for local economic regeneration and small business development.

Voluntary organisations
Finally, local voluntary sector bodies, including religious institutions, could become EM members. Voluntary organisations could draw on the EM's diverse membership to harness support for voluntary work in the local area. Members of an EM might decide, for example, to undertake local environmental projects or to help old people in the community, providing valuable work experience for unemployed members in the process. It would be vital for the EM to have a wider social life beyond its narrow economic task and a sense of social as well as economic purpose.

The EM would be created by this joint investment of money, effort, skills and services in kind by local people, businesses, voluntary groups and the local authority, in order to pool risks, generate mutual gains and deliver services. Of course, it would all need to add up. A business plan and three-year budget set out in the appendix show how a notional mutual could become financially self-sustaining within three years.

3.3 What members would get out of an EM
The EM would provide a range of services to its members. Some would be services in kind provided by mutual members to one another. Other services would mainly be financed by cash payments from members who could afford to pay, including employers. The mutual would also deliver public training and economic development programmes, of which only some members of the mutual (typically the unemployed) might be eligible beneficiaries.

The mutual would support members throughout the 'life-cycle' of their involvement in the labour market. It would provide them with a durable relationship, amid the turbulence of modern flexible work. The mutual would provide an unemployed person, for example, with preparation to re-enter employment, such as literacy and numeracy training. It would then help the person to find work through job search initiatives. If necessary, the EM would help to arrange childcare for them, or deliver it directly. If the person lost their job, they would turn back to the EM for support, advice on reapplying for benefits and social contact to prevent them becoming isolated from the world of work. If the job lasted, the mutual would continue to help with childcare and offer the member opportunities to improve their skills. This life-cycle relationship between the EM and a job seeking member is set out in Figure 3. A schematic list of the services the EM would provide to different members and how they would be financed is set out in Figure 4.

Working members and employer members would be charged for many of the EM's services, but these would be less expensive than elsewhere. Services in kind provided primarily by members would reduce the mutual's costs and the diverse membership of the mutual would find ways of combining its resources cost effectively. Any membership fees in excess of the mutual's basic running costs could also be spent to finance services for members.

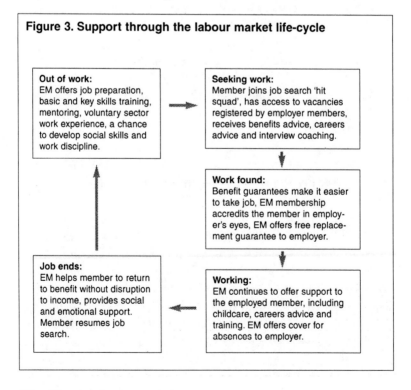

Figure 3. Support through the labour market life-cycle

Out of work:
EM offers job preparation, basic and key skills training, mentoring, voluntary sector work experience, a chance to develop social skills and work discipline.

Seeking work:
Member joins job search 'hit squad', has access to vacancies registered by employer members, receives benefits advice, careers advice and interview coaching.

Work found:
Benefit guarantees make it easier to take job, EM membership accredits the member in employer's eyes, EM offers free replacement guarantee to employer.

Job ends:
EM helps member to return to benefit without disruption to income, provides social and emotional support. Member resumes job search.

Working:
EM continues to offer support to the employed member, including childcare, careers advice and training. EM offers cover for absences to employer.

Figure 4. Services the EM would provide for its members

Service	Target Members	Organisation/Funding
Job search	Unemployed	Self-help job search 'hit squads'
Job placement	Businesses, esp. small businesses	EM service with quality & money-back guarantees Employers charged
Applicant accreditation	Job seekers	EM & mentors validate job-readiness of members
Job broking	Part-time/temporary workers	EM job-broker puts together job packages
Training	All members	Public funding Charges
Childcare	All members	Qualified full-time workers organise cooperative self-help Parents and employers charged
Community contract work	Long-term unemployed Economically inactive	With local voluntary sector taskforces etc.
Benefits advice	People moving into/out of jobs	Trained members help one another through benefit system
Benefits flexibility	People moving into/out of jobs	Special rules for EM ease transition between benefits and work
Financial services	All members	Mature EM creates credit union, delivers consumer services and other financial products
Business networks	Self-employed Small businesses	Business support services Mature EM brokers cooperative approaches to training and technology

Whereas relationships between employers and employees are becoming more transitory in the modern labour market, the relationship between an EM and its members would be durable and dependable. That continuity would be based on the EM's ability to provide relevant services to its members. A mature EM would provide at least the following services:

Job search
The mutual would organise concerted job search. Members would not just look for work on their own or for themselves. The mutual would organise job 'hit squads' to scour the local area for work on behalf of all members. This coordinated job search would be more efficient than the approach adopted by most public programmes, which provide some job-search training and then encourage the person to search on their own. A survey conducted for the Department for Education and Employment in 1995 found that on average unemployed people spend about six and a half hours a week on job search and applications. In a mutual, they would be expected to look harder and to search for the EM as a whole, canvassing employers for work and creating a pool of EM vacancies open to all members.

Job placement
The EM would offer employers a cost-effective job placement service; this would be a natural counterpart to the job search service described above. The EM would be more attractive to employers than the Employment Service as it would have a better understanding of its job-seeking members' skills and of local employers' needs. The mutual would offer employers quality guarantees, including a money-back policy if a placement did not work out and a guarantee to provide a replacement free-of-charge if the first EM candidate proved unsuitable. This would enable employers to recruit from among the unemployed at low risk. At the same time, the mutual would be less expensive than a private agency, because its running costs would be lower: much of the job-search, matching and administrative functions would be pro-

vided by members as services in kind, working with a small core staff. The mutual would also provide after-placement services such as temporary cover for holidays or childcare-related breaks, and personal support from a member-mentor. This support would help local employers to reduce absenteeism and staff turnover.

A particularly valuable role for this job placement service might be to bring together employers and disabled jobseekers. Employers are often put off employing disabled workers by inaccurate perceptions of the risks and costs involved. An EM would help to reduce these perceived risks by providing employers with more job-ready disabled candidates and helping both parties through the issues they would need to tackle. The EM would help its disabled members to access work and provide local employers with a valuable resource: a trained and employable group of disabled workers. This would help employers to meet their obligations under disability discrimination law. This is just one example of how the EM could help employers and jobseekers to solve what are ultimately mutual problems.

Job accreditation
One of the biggest obstacles the unemployed face in getting back into employment is to persuade employers of their work discipline, inter-personal skills and motivation. The EM would help to address this. The membership covenant would stress that someone had to fulfil their responsibilities to the mutual, to look for work and to help other members. Membership of the mutual, therefore, would in itself signal work-readiness, motivation and commitment. The mutual would be an advocate for its jobseeking members, and the value of the mutual's brand would increase as it built up a track record of reliable service to employers. The involvement of businesses would be vital, for instance in helping to design training programmes and job search initiatives.

Job packages
For people working part time who wanted to work longer hours, the mutual could help to package together two or more part-time

jobs, liaising with the employers. Alternatively, it could create a package which combined a part-time job with training, volunteering or the provision of services in kind to the mutual. The EM could make it easier for members to vary their activities across weeks or months, structuring their work lives in a way that suited them. For example, the EM could arrange for an employed member to take study leave by providing the employer with a temporary replacement.

Training
The EM would deliver training courses, ranging from basic skills training for the unemployed to more advanced programmes for employed members. These might be delivered by the members themselves, using a range of public funds, including New Deal, TEC funding, the Single Regeneration Budget and European Union finance. Employed members would be expected to cover some of the costs of their training. The mutual would also provide cost-effective training for businesses, particularly micro-firms, which often find it difficult to provide training for their employees. A mutual could bring small firms together to address their common training needs and find cooperative solutions. The EM could also work with larger employers to come up with cost-effective ways of delivering training: for example, employers could make available to mutual members any surplus places on their in-house courses. The involvement of employers would help the mutual to ensure that its training was relevant to the local labour market. The mutual movement could also develop in tandem with the University for Industry, to provide members with a framework for lifelong learning.

Childcare
The EM would train its members to provide childcare for other members, building upon informal networks of childcare to provide crèche services and a full-time nursery. Childcare services would be open to employed members, unemployed members (such as lone parents) looking for work and businesses that want-

ed to provide their employees with access to childcare. As well as addressing the shortage of supply of childcare, the mutual would develop innovative ways of spreading its cost. Unemployed members could help to provide childcare in exchange for training or help with job search, while employed members and employers would pay towards the costs. The mutual might join forces with a large employer to set up a nursery to be used by members of both organisations.

Voluntary community work
The mutual would help people to maintain contact with work by organising voluntary work initiatives. The EM would be a mechanism through which neighbourhood groups, religious institutions, environmental groups and charities combined to create voluntary work programmes for unemployed members. These volunteering networks might acquire greater importance during a recession. The mutual's flexibility and close links with the local community would enable it to adapt its activities according to the economic cycle.

Benefits advice
One of the most daunting aspects of moving from unemployment into employment and back again is the confusing array of benefit rules. The EM would help its new members through this jungle, by training longer-standing members to advise them. Most disabled workers, for example, become disabled during the course of their life. The EM could help them through the maze of assessments and benefits they will face. Often it takes a newly disabled worker nine months to receive benefits after first applying for them; the EM could support them through this period.

Benefits flexibility
In addition to these services, members of the EM would benefit from modified benefit rules. These modifications would improve the incentives for members to take work, including part-time or temporary jobs, and would make the transition from welfare to

work less disruptive. Members would be entitled to these privileges by virtue of their commitment to work enshrined in their covenant and the mutual's internal discipline (see Section 5.1 below). A number of possible ways to spring the benefit traps which make it difficult for people to move into jobs are outlined in Chapter 4.

Networks for the self-employed
The EM would provide business services for self-employed homeworkers, who are poorly catered for. Initially, the EM could provide them with office back-up: printing, photocopying, message services and meeting rooms. A more ambitious goal would be for the mutual to create networks of self-employed people, to allow them to share tips and support one another. This might be particularly relevant for disabled homeworkers. The EM could help them to create a self-help network and to purchase on better terms the adaptive equipment they might need to work from home. An example of how such networks might develop is the Sustainable Strength self-help organisation being launched in Birmingham to help Asian women to become self-employed. This development stems in part from self-help initiatives in the Indian sub-continent such as the Grameen Bank. Another initiative has been launched in Huddersfield to create a mutual organisation for self-employed teleworkers.

Other services
The EM's core services would all be work-related, but a mature mutual could expand its activities. One area would be financial services for members. An EM could establish itself as a credit union. By entering into a joint venture with a bank or building society, the mutual could also provide mortgages or insurance to people who often find it difficult to access such services. The mutual could gather the purchasing power of members to win discounts from local firms. Another possible role for the mutual would be a broker of networks for small businesses. There is already a scheme of this kind, run by a British company called

BusinessNet, which creates networks through which like-minded firms can address shared needs to upgrade their technology or skills. The EM would become a key partner in local economic development initiatives, most of which are targeted at small businesses.

Social life

The EM would not succeed if it were a purely economic institution. It would also need to be held together by a social life. This could range from organising social and entertainment events, to social projects such as local environmental work and community care. As well as providing members with services, the mutual would offer members a sense of belonging which comes from membership of a living organisation. Members of the mutual would always have somewhere to turn when times were tough.

4. Easing the transition from benefits to work

The EM would create a more effective way for jobseekers and local employers to find one other. By providing unemployed members with support, it would improve their chances of moving into work. But the EM would also provide a way round the barriers to work created by the benefit system. EM members would benefit from modified benefit rules, which would improve incentives to take work and reduce the insecurity people suffer during the transition into work. The Government would be a sleeping partner in the mutual: it would reward mutual members' commitment to work with benefit rules to make it easier for them to mix income from employment with benefits. The self-imposed internal discipline of the mutual would minimise the risk of anyone 'taking advantage' of these modified rules. The mutual would be an honest broker between the state and the claimant, an intermediary which would lubricate not just the labour market but also the benefit system as well.

The establishment of the first EMs would provide an opportunity for piloting novel approaches to springing benefit traps. Three are suggested here. The first two involve changes to the way in which benefits are paid. In the third, the EM would employ some of its members, taking them off unemployment benefits altogether. These options are set out schematically in Figure 5 opposite.

Benefit guarantees
Upon joining the EM, unemployed members would be given four benefit guarantees. First, the EM would guarantee to help the members claim their full entitlement to benefits, including in-work benefits. Benefit rules for people in employment are complex. Many jobseekers do not know what benefits they might be entitled to when they have a job. This particularly applies to Housing Benefit. An unemployed person needs to make a new application for Housing Benefit when they get a job. As many do not, they reduce their potential in-work income.

Figure 5. Benefit guarantees and flexibility the EM might provide

Offer	Aim
EM helps members claim full in-work benefit entitlement, including Housing Benefit	Raise in-work income to make work more attractive
EM sanctioned to pay in-work benefits until Benefits Agency/ Inland Revenue pays	Avoid delays that create costly disruptions to income, ease transition from unemployment into work
EM sanctioned to pay out-of-work benefits from day one of unemployment	Minimise disruptions to income caused by cycling between work and unemployment, reduce fear of taking a job
Member guaranteed to return to old benefit levels if job lost	Minimise disruptions to income caused by moving between work and unemployment, reduce fear of taking a job
EM 'flexible benefits' scheme (guaranteed minimum income)	Allow EM members to mix income from part-time and temporary work with benefits
EM as an employer	EM to employ some members and contract out their services to local employers, moving the members out of unemployment altogether

Second, the EM would guarantee that in-work benefits would be paid from day one of a member moving into employment. Often when someone unemployed takes a job, their in-work benefits are not paid for several weeks as their entitlement is assessed, and this risk discourages some people from taking work. The EM would bridge this gap by making in-work benefit payments until the Benefits Agency and (with the introduction of the Working Families Tax Credit) the Inland Revenue had made their assessments. The EM would be sanctioned to perform this role by these agencies, which would cover the expense. In essence, the EM would help its unemployed members through the 'cashflow' crisis they might face when they get a job.

Third, the EM would guarantee that out-of-work benefits would be paid from day one to a member returning to unemployment after losing a job. When someone becomes unemployed again, perhaps after a brief spell in employment, they have to go through a series of bureaucratic hoops to claim their benefits. Delays in receiving benefits can cause great hardship and fear of this disruption can be a significant factor that deters people from taking jobs. The EM would overcome this fear by guaranteeing to pay out-of-work benefits from day one of unemployment. Again, this would depend on the EM being sanctioned to do this by the Benefits Agency and the Employment Service.

Fourth, the EM would guarantee to members that if they did have to return to out-of-work benefits, they would return to their original level of entitlement. In some cases, benefit claimants who take and then lose a job find that their benefit entitlement is reduced as a consequence of the period of employment, a danger which further increases the insecurity of moving into work.

These four guarantees would reduce the uncertainty and risk which discourage many claimants from taking work. None of this would require higher public spending – it would simply mean licensing the EM to act as an intermediary between the big bureaucracies of the state, the Inland Revenue and the Benefits Agency, and the claimant.

The administration of the guarantees would have to be simple. The level of detail involved in conducting a means test would be beyond the mutual; Department of Social Security staff are trained for fifteen weeks before conducting their first assessment. To avoid this complexity, the EM's guarantees could be delivered in one of two ways. First, the relevant agencies would licence the EM to conduct an interim estimate of the member's benefit entitlement; the EM would be able to make payments for a limited period only and up to a capped amount. Alternatively, the EM would be authorised to pay a flat-rate bridging benefit during transitions from welfare to work or back again.

The benefit guarantees would not make it any easier for members to take part-time jobs of less than sixteen hours per week, as such jobs do not lift a claimant off Jobseeker's Allowance or Income Support. People in this situation see their benefit withdrawn pound-for-pound for all earnings over a small 'disregard'. It would help mutual members to take occasional part-time jobs if they benefited from more generous disregards and were able to 'bank' them from week to week.

Flexible benefits

The flexible benefits package would be designed to help EM members mix income from part-time and temporary work with income from benefits. The EM would take the weekly benefit entitlement of the member upon joining the mutual as a baseline figure for a minimum hourly income for a 35-hour week. A benefit entitlement of £40 per week, for example, would result in a minimum income of £1.14 per hour. The member would be paid this amount for those hours in the week in which they were not working. For example, suppose the member got a part-time job for fifteen hours a week, paying £4 an hour. Their weekly wage would be £60 plus twenty hours worth of benefits, at £1.14 an hour, giving a total weekly income of £83.

The EM would pay the minimum income to the member according to the hours, days or weeks in which the member was not in work. The member referred to above might find a fixed-term full-time job for four weeks, during which time they would receive no benefit. They might then have to wait for a week without any work; for that week, they would receive the full minimum income. If they then returned to their part-time job, they would again receive twenty hours of flexible benefits per week. The EM would charge these payments to the Benefits Agency and/or the Employment Service.

Flexible benefits would make it much easier for members to take part-time or temporary jobs, as long as they did not depend on in-work benefits to make work pay. For those with high benefit entitlements, an amount corresponding to in-work benefits would have to be paid on top of each hour's pay received, although this would be complex to administer. A simpler alternative would be to offer flexible benefits only to those working less than sixteen hours per week, who do not qualify for in-work benefits, and to use the four benefit guarantees to help those moving into jobs with longer hours.

The EM could also provide a vehicle for pilots of radical alternatives to the present benefits regime, such as a negative income tax or a Citizen's Income.

The EM as employer
A third option would be for the EM to employ some of its members. The contract might stipulate a 35-hour week at the prevailing minimum wage for one year. Employed members would be eligible for in-work benefits and tax credits in the usual fashion and would be contracted out to work on assignment with local employers, in the way that agency temporaries are. For each hour they worked on assignment, the members would receive the minimum wage, plus a premium which would reward the member for the assignment. The EM would retain the balance between the amount paid to the member (minimum wage plus premium) and the charge to the employer, and use it to help cover the wage bill in down-times. If the members' assignments did not occupy 35 hours in any given week, they would make up the difference by providing services to the mutual, for which they would receive the minimum wage only. This arrangement would require a special contract to be drawn up between the EM and the member. It could be administratively complicated to begin with, but it would have the attraction of taking the member off the unemployment register altogether.

5. The employee mutual in practice

The task of taking the employee mutual from the drawing board into practice raises three main issues. First, how would an EM have to be organised, in practice, to ensure it was sustainable? Second, how would the EM be financed? Third, what sort of legislative and regulatory framework should govern the EM and its relations with organisations such as Training and Enterprise Councils?

5.1 Internal organisation

The EM should be able to draw upon the experience of a range of local mutual institutions in the UK, such as credit unions, housing associations, friendly societies and Local Exchange Trading Schemes (or LETs), in which people trade services in kind by using vouchers. Members of LETs schemes are given quarterly statements of how much they have put into the scheme and as a result how much they have to spend on other members' services. The Muslim and the Afro-Caribbean communities in the UK, for example, have resilient mutual savings institutions, which provide interesting lessons. The EM movement could also draw upon the experience of membership organisations from abroad, including time-dollar volunteering schemes in the US and self-help networks among self-employed workers in the Indian sub-continent. Lessons could be learned from micro-credit initiatives such as Credal in Belgium, Adie in France and Fundusz Mikro in Poland as well as Working Capital in Massachusetts, Women's SELF in Chicago, Illinois, and the Grameen and SEWA Banks in India. In the UK, at least three projects may have lessons for the employee mutual: the Women's Enterprise, Employment and Training Unit in Norwich, which has established a loan fund for the self-employed; the Wellpark Enterprise Centre in Glasgow; and the Sustainable Strength Network in Birmingham. A far from exhaustive survey of the experience of mutual institutions such as these suggests that an employee mutual will have to address the following issues to be a success.

Scale

An EM that was too small would not be sustainable. Many LETs trading schemes have no more than 50 members and are often too small to thrive. A credit union can survive if it has 500-plus members, but to be sustainable it needs more like 2,000 members. Many credit unions are merging in order to computerise and maintain a small paid staff. For the EM to offer a recruitment service to local employers it will need a sizeable pool of job-seeking members; this is another area where there are important economies of scale. A membership of about 2,000 seems a reasonable start-up target for an EM.

Mixed membership

An EM will need a mixed membership, to bring the unemployed into contact with the mainstream jobs market, enabling them to network with employers and employees. It needs to bring employers into contact with potential recruits. To be successful, an EM would have to be capable of reaching, socially and geographically, beyond areas of high unemployment. If an EM covered too small an area, for instance a run down housing estate or a very poor neighbourhood, it would not reach into more affluent markets where people might find work.

It would be advisable to pilot several different kinds of mutual, with different memberships. An EM dedicated to a particular group would be able to tailor its services to the needs of that group and might also find it easier to generate a sense of mutual interest. Examples could include: a lone mothers' EM to cover a city, focused on a nursery and other childcare services; an EM for ex-service personnel to cover a large conurbation; an EM for disabled homeworkers, operating over the Internet; or an EM run by and for an extended religious community. There is a different but equally valid case to be made for an EM with open membership: an inclusive EM might be better able to promote local labour market efficiency and social cohesion.

Institutional base
Local mutual institutions stand a better chance of survival if they can use a strong institution to provide their foundations. It is not impossible to get mutual institutions up and running from scratch. But the task is easier if the mutual can 'piggy-back' on another institution. One explanation for the growth of credit unions in rural Ireland was the strength of the Catholic Church when most of them were set up. Muslim bond committees in the UK are durable, in part, because most are based around a Mosque. In the UK, the strongest credit unions are those organised around employers, such as local authorities and police forces. An EM could be hosted by a company, a school, a religious institution or a library. It should not be hosted by the local authority or the Employment Service, as this would identify it with the public sector.

In some cases, it might be appropriate for successful mutual organisations operating in other fields, such as credit unions, or other local institutions which are already involved in economic development, such as development trusts, to foster an EM. However, given the tendency for local economic associations, committees and partnerships to proliferate it is vital that the EM should have a distinct identity and a clear set of objectives, focused on its core work-related and employment-related services.

Social entrepreneurship
An EM will require a motivating social entrepreneur to drive it forward, with a core team of supporters. A social entrepreneur is someone who uses skills and techniques borrowed from business to create a social institution capable of generating lasting social value. Mutual institutions depend on involving their members and volunteers, but it is difficult to get them going and to sustain them without the drive of a team of ambitious innovative social entrepreneurs. One role for large companies would be to sponsor social entrepreneurs. For example, if all the companies listed in the FTSE 250 were each to sponsor one social entrepreneur for three years to create an EM of 2,000 people, the EM movement

could soon cover half a million people. This would be a practical way for large companies to reinvest in local social and economic infrastructure.

Legal structure

The legal structure will need to capture the spirit of mutuality and membership but allow the EM to act in an entrepreneurial manner. The best way would be to create a set of rules that each EM would adopt. These would be drawn up by a national sponsoring body for employee mutuals. These rules would cover the central organisational structure: membership, ownership rights, governance and management responsibilities. One possibility would be for the EM to be an industrial and provident society, regulated by the Registrar of Friendly Societies, which covers credit unions, cooperatives and friendly societies. A better approach would be for an EM to be a company limited by guarantee, with a constitution which allowed for different kinds of membership. This would allow companies to be members of the EM, something not possible for friendly societies. The EM, as a company limited by guarantee, could draw upon the collateral of its corporate members to raise loans from a bank to start up its operation.

The EM would be owned by its members, who would have the right to change the constitution and approve the accounts. They would elect the board, which would appoint the chairman. The board membership would change each year, with perhaps 25 per cent of board seats up for election each year. The EM would have to decide how to distribute any financial surplus on its trading activities. One possibility would be for the surplus to be distributed to its members; the other would be for the surplus to be reinvested in the mutual. It is vital that the EM should be structured so that members feel it is their organisation: something they have to take responsibility for and will benefit from.

Discipline

The employee mutual will need to deal with members who flout the rules, for instance by bringing the EM into disrepute or by persistently free-riding on the efforts of other members. The EM must be professional and well-run, with members taking responsibility for their relations with one another; it cannot be a soft option.

The EM would impose work discipline in a quite different way from either the state or private sector employers. One attraction of mutual organisations, in theory at least, is that they require less formal management because they rely on peer review and a sense of mutual obligation: authority within the mutual should be self-imposed.

This spirit of collective self-discipline is evident in the most impressive credit unions, which adopt a problem-solving approach to arrears. Problems of poor payment in credit unions are often due to poor communication or undisclosed financial difficulties which members are too ashamed to talk about. Often they can be solved by renegotiating the terms of a loan and finding new ways to involve members. This problem-solving approach is time consuming but it maintains the cohesion of the union: free-riding is not allowed, but people who slip into arrears are not excluded. Only if this problem-solving approach fails, do credit unions bring in debt collectors.

The EM's first response to problems, such as non-performance of services in kind, would be to attempt to negotiate a solution. Sanctions, such as suspension or expulsion, would only be used as a last resort. The EM would address the balance between rights and responsibilities in an entirely new light: by joining an EM, members would be endorsing a sense of collective self-discipline and an ethic of cooperative self-improvement.

Launch and set-up
The launch of an EM in a locality will be critical to give it momentum and credibility. Each mutual would be guided by a model launch strategy, which would include press material, advertising and branding, advice on winning and publicising endorsements from local politicians, business leaders and the like.

It would perhaps take six months to get an EM ready to take in its first members. The social entrepreneur appointed to create the EM in an area would be given three months to gather together a core group of supporters in business, politics and the voluntary sector. The mutual would be launched after a further three months of intensive development. The core group of members would launch a six-month membership drive in the area, offering 1,000 places initially. People would need to commit themselves to the mutual, otherwise there would be a danger that membership might be devalued. After the first 1,000 places had been filled, the EM would aim to recruit the next 1,000-plus members during the second year. This time-scale would have to be revised for rural areas, where employee mutuals would need to take distinctive forms.

5.2 Financial viability

Although a mutual might recruit a membership of 2,000 within two years, it would take longer for it to become trusted and established. Evidence from other mutual institutions suggests that it takes three to five years before a mutual organisation commands respect and trust from all those who might join it or use its services. The EM would need to start with a three-year funding commitment from sponsoring organisations to give it a chance of succeeding. Otherwise, too much effort would be taken up by fundraising in the early stages of the organisation's development.

A business plan and projected three-year budget for a notional employee mutual is set out in the appendix. This shows that a mutual which grew to have 2,500 individual members within three years would be financially viable, as long as it had the right mix of members and its start-up costs were covered from public funds, corporate donations and its own fundraising. The assumptions underpinning the budget would of course have to be tested at the pilot stage.

The first of those assumptions is that the mutual would have little or no membership income in year one. Between year one and year three its membership would grow to 2,500. Initially, about 10 per cent of the members would be self-employed, about 30 per cent would be employed and the remainder would be unemployed; the proportion of unemployed members would fall as the mutual helped them to move into work. Large business membership would grow from 20 in the first year, to 30 by year three, while small business membership would rise from 40 in the first year to 100 in year three. Income from this membership has been projected on the basis of a higher and lower rate of contributions. At the higher rate, the self-employed and employed would pay £5 a week to join the club, large businesses would pay £20 per week and small businesses £7. At the lower rate, the self-employed and employed would pay £3 per week, large businesses £15 and small businesses £5. Unemployed members would pay 50p per week and put in at least fifteen hours of services in kind.

This budget (summarised in Figure 6) is no more than a general outline, but it shows that the EM could more than cover its basic running costs through membership fees after its first two or three years.

Figure 6. Summary of projected three year budget			
	Launch Year One	Year Two	Year Three
Costs (£)	209,600	234,925	241,967
Income from Membership Fees (£)			
@ Higher Rate Contributions	0	241,280	396,240
@ Lower Rate Contributions	0	153,400	249,600

5.3 The external framework for the EM

An EM will prosper only in a supportive legislative and regulatory environment. The EM would need political endorsement, at national and local level, to confer legitimacy on the innovation and to help manage the risks involved. The environment for the EM would be most influenced by central government policy. For an EM to embed itself as a local institution, however, the mutual would also need to develop strong local partnerships and relationships. The EM must not be seen as just another invention of central government policy, but as a genuinely local institution, addressing local needs.

(i) The national framework
Developing a constructive framework for the EM will require high levels of cooperation between and support from government departments. It will involve at least these ingredients:

Benefits regulations Benefit rules must be modified for EM members, to allow them to access as wide a range of work opportunities as possible. The Benefits Agency and Employment Service would have to licence the EM to make interim assessments of benefit entitlement. With the introduction of the Working Families Tax Credit, a similar relationship would also be needed with the Inland Revenue.

Employment law By charging employers for filling their vacancies, or by employing members directly and charging out their time, the EM might fall within the regulatory regime in place for employment agencies. These regulations are under review by the current government.

Taxation The EM would not be a charity, but it would have a social purpose – to provide members with security and support, and to make local labour markets function more efficiently. Thus it should be eligible for more favourable tax treatment than the average company. People and organisations that trade with the

EM should gain some tax advantages. Corporate investment in the EM, for instance to sponsor the work of the social entrepreneur, might be tax deductible. Interest on corporate loans to an EM might be tax deductible. Mutual trade within the EM's membership might be tax free.

Public funds The EM should be eligible to receive public funds from a variety of sources, including state-funded employment and training programmes under the New Deal, TEC programmes and funding for small business development through the Business Links scheme (for example for coordinating a cooperative approach to training and development among local firms). The EM would also be eligible for funding from the Single Regeneration Budget and from the European Union.

Regulation An EM would need to meet the highest standards of probity, as it would be using public funds, handling its members' money and working closely with government agencies to make benefit and tax credit assessments. The first line of regulation to ensure probity should be the EM's board and the EM's independent auditors. There should also be a national system of auditing, however. Rather than create a separate auditor specifically for the EM, the best approach might be for the Audit Commission to audit EMs, covering both their financial probity and effectiveness. The Commission already has considerable expertise in this area.

National leadership A national body would accredit and represent local employee mutuals. This national council of employee mutuals would: be the custodian of the rules that each EM would adopt; provide back-up when a new EM was being launched; gather and spread best practice; provide advice and consultancy; and promote the movement nationally and lobby for it in Whitehall. The credit union movement has been hamstrung by a leadership divided between two national organisations. The EM movement should avoid a similar fate.

(ii) The local framework
Each EM would have to be rooted in strong local relationships:

Local politics The EM will need to develop relationships with community leaders, councillors and church leaders, who are capable of winning local recognition and legitimacy for the new institution.

Local authorities The EM should not be seen as an off-shoot of the local authority as that would undermine its independence and the members' sense of ownership. Yet a successful EM will need to establish a good working relationship with the relevant local authority, working in tandem with its economic development plans. One possibility would be for the EM to become a vehicle for local authority economic development initiatives.

Regional development authorities One important role for RDAs might be to promote the development and cross-fertilisation of the EMs within their regions.

TECs / LECs The employee mutual's work would overlap with that of the Training and Enterprise Councils (Local Enterprise Companies in Scotland). Both would be charged with assessing and providing for local training needs, in part by giving employers a voice in designing training provision. Yet the employee mutuals would differ quite markedly from the TECs. The EM would be a local institution, with a strong, mixed membership, whereas TECs tend to cover a large area, with a looser membership, drawn from business. Some TECs are creative and innovative, but many have failed to break free from the influence of the tripartite training system that they replaced. The best outcome would be for the TECs and the mutuals to work in partnership. There would be no sense in an EM attempting to replace a TEC that was working well. On the other hand, some TECs seem to be ineffective; the development of employee mutuals should not be constrained by them.

Figure 7. Internal and external factors to make the EM a success

Issues	Comments
Scale	Need 2,000-plus membership to be viable
Membership balance	Need mix of members: unemployed, employed, businesses, self-employed
Foundations	In many cases, build EM on an existing base: credit union, religious institution, voluntary organisation, company
Legal structure	Company limited by guarantee, with membership
Governance	Board elected by membership
Management & leadership	Development led by social entrepreneur and core supporters Mature mutual led by entrepreneurial chief executive answerable to board
Finance/funding	Public funding for some start-up costs Membership fees Public funding for training Charges for services ie recruitment, childcare, training Services in kind
Discipline	Members commit by signing covenant Clear disciplinary procedures, starting with peer advice/problem solving. Sanctions (eg suspension, expulsion) used as last resort
Audit/regulation	Independent auditors backed up by Audit Commission.
National framework	EM allowed special benefits regime. Eligible for public funding, pump-priming, tax advantages. National Council of Employee Mutuals to promote national development drive.

Trade unions The EM would not be a trade union. In many respects, the EM is a response to the weakness of trade unions, which have found it difficult, or have not been interested in, recruiting among the unemployed and the self-employed, young people and women, especially those employed in small businesses in the service sector. The EM would be tailored to meet the needs of people that trade unions have traditionally not touched. Nevertheless, it is important that trade unions should not feel threatened by the development of the EM initiative or stand in its way.

Voluntary organisations The EM would have to team up with local voluntary organisations to: recruit members; cooperate on joint work-related projects; develop local legitimacy and roots; pull in caring services that the EM might need to access for its members; and provide opportunities for EM members to gain work experience through volunteering.

6. Next steps

The employee mutual is not an abstract idea; *it is a concrete proposal to create a durable and relevant institution at the heart of the flexible labour market.* Initially, it would be vital to pilot the employee mutual in different labour markets and with different memberships. These pilots could be launched next year, and would need to run for two to three years before they could be properly evaluated. Assuming they were successful, a five-year nationwide programme could be launched in 2002, aiming to establish 250 employee mutuals, each with an individual membership of 2,000, within five years. That would mean that within less than a decade from now there would be close to half a million members of the employee mutual movement, with tens of thousands of associate members in the companies which became corporate members.

Below is a rough timetable for creating a national movement of employee mutuals over the next ten years.

1998: Raise public and private sponsorship to create 25 pilot employee mutuals and recruit social entrepreneurs to run them. Win political, business and voluntary backing for the initiative.

1999: Set up the 25 pilots across the UK in a range of social and economic settings, dealing with different sorts of labour markets and client groups, to test the model.

2002: Complete the evaluation of the pilots according to their success at their core tasks: to recruit and retain members, provide services to individual members and local employers, and move unemployed people into work. Use this assessment to refine the model. Launch a national programme, organised by the newly created national council of employee mutuals, to create 250 employee mutuals, each with 2,000 members, by the year 2007. Give the national council performance targets for growth and quality standards. This national programme would need to be led by a team of entrepreneurs with a sense of mission, marketing and political skills.

2004: Assess the performance of the first batch of employee mutuals. Assuming they were successful, set higher targets for the number and membership of employee mutuals beyond 2007.

2005: The most successful mutuals would be in a position to develop a wider range of financial and consumer services.

2010: The employee mutual should be fully accepted as a fundamental feature of the modern labour market, alongside other institutions such as trade unions, the Employment Service and recruitment agencies.

7. Conclusion

The Job Club started as a pilot project in a Birmingham voluntary organisation in the early 1980s. Now there are hundreds of Job Clubs up and down the country. Training and Enterprise Councils developed in the UK from the mid-1980s after the then Manpower Services Commission borrowed from the experience of Employer Councils in US cities. Over the next decade, the employee mutual could also grow from the pilot stage to become an accepted part of working life for thousands of people and companies. It would be a distinctive, durable response to the pressures created by the flexible labour market. We are in the midst of a period of rapid economic and technological innovation. We need to match our investment in such innovation with a similar investment in social institutions to help people cope with and benefit from change.

The aim of the employee mutual is *to combine flexibility with security*. That will only be possible if we create new institutions of cooperative self-help, which allow people to exert more control over their lives, reduce uncertainty, share risk and create opportunities for self-improvement. The state can help with that task, but it is often distrusted for being overly bureaucratic and distant. Its services are sometimes regarded as irrelevant and intrusive, in part because people do not see public services as something that they are responsible for or have a stake in.

People would have a stake in their employee mutual. Members would create their own cooperative solutions to shared problems. Drawing on this self-help ethic, the employee mutual would be a contemporary institution, designed to address contemporary problems. By working with the grain of the flexible labour market, it would enable members to manage the risks of flexibility and make the most of the opportunities it offers.

Appendix: budget and business plan for a model employee mutual

This budget and business plan takes the employee mutual through the first three years of its life to a position of financial stability. It shows how the mutual would be able to cover its basic costs from membership fees and would therefore be self-sufficient. The financing of services provided to members is considered at the end of the appendix.

1. Membership recruitment and growth
We assume the employee mutual's first three years will be divided into these phases.

0 – 6 months Planning and development. Recruitment of local partners/sponsors. Advisory board appointed. Core staff, facilities and initial services – job search, job placement, childcare – put in place.

6 – 12 months Intensive membership recruitment drive for first 1,000 individual members.

Membership mix :	60% unemployed
	10% self-employed
	30% employed
Recruitment target:	166 people per month
Recruit:	20 large business members
	40 small business members

12 – 18 months

Recruitment targets:	Take individual members to 1,500
Membership mix:	56% unemployed
	12% self-employed
	32% employed

Take business membership to:
25 large business members
60 small business members

18 – 24 months	Recruitment targets:	Take individual members to 2,000
	Membership mix:	52% unemployed
		14% self-employed
		34% employed
	Take business membership to:	
		30 large business members
		80 small business members

24 – 30 months	Recruitment targets:	Take individual members to 2,250
	Membership mix :	48% unemployed
		16% self-employed
		36% employed
	Take business membership to:	
		30 large business members
		90 small business members

30 – 36 months	Recruitment targets:	Take individual members to 2,500
	Membership mix:	44% unemployed
		18% self-employed
		38% employed
	Take business membership to:	
		30 large business members
		100 small business members

2. Membership fees

The employee mutual's income from membership fees would depend on: the size of its membership; the mix of members (unemployed, employed and self-employed, businesses of various sizes); and the rate set for members' fees. For simplicity, we assume that businesses are either 'small' or 'large'. In practice, business contributions might be based on a sliding scale related to turnover.

The budget is based on two illustrative levels of charges. At the higher level, self-employed and employed members would be charged £5 per week; large businesses would pay £20 and small businesses £7 per week. At the lower level, self-employed and employed members would be charged £3 per week, large businesses £10 and small businesses £5 per week. We assume that unemployed members would pay 50p per week to be a member of the mutual.

The table below sets out the EM's potential income from membership fees, over three years, at both the higher and lower contribution rates, assuming the mix of membership set out in the business plan above. We assume that the EM would receive no income from membership fees during its first year.

Potential income from membership fees

| | | | | Income from membership fees | |
Months into Development	Individual Members	Large Businesses	Small Businesses	Higher Rate(£)	Lower Rate(£)
0	-	-	-	-	-
6	-	-	-	-	-
12	1,000	20	40	154,960	98,800
18	1,500	25	60	241,280	153,400
24	2,000	30	80	336,960	213,200
30	2,250	30	90	396,240	249,600
36	2,500	30	100	460,200	288,600

3. Costs

We separate the EM's costs into launch costs to get the organisation up and running, and running costs.

We assume that the launch phase will last one year and that during this period the EM will have no members and no income. We also assume that the launch costs (all the costs incurred during the first year) will be non-recoverable and will therefore have to be financed using funds from outside the mutual.

Running costs are all costs incurred from the second year onwards, by when the EM is fully staffed and has a substantial membership.

(a) Launch costs
We assume the employee mutual will incur the following launch costs during its start-up phase (year one).

Launch costs (year one)

Staff

EM chief executive/social entrepreneur	£27,000
Job search/placement coordinator	£20,500
Child care coordinator	£20,500
Benefits coordinator	£20,500
Administrative support	£14,000
	£102,500
Plus NI/pensions @ 16%	*£118,900*
Advertising, marketing, induction	*£25,000*

General costs

Rent	£7,000
Postage, photocopying, stationery, telephone	£5,000
Travel	£1,500
Equipment, furniture etc.	£15,000
Computers	£20,000
Financial management, auditing, insurance	£10,200
Sundry	£4,000
Staff training/away days	£3,000
Total general costs	*£65,700*
Total launch costs	**£209,600**

These launch costs would have to be funded from non-recurring income. This income would primarily be contributions from large businesses and public funds. The latter could come from various existing sources but might also include core funding. Possible sources of income to cover these start-up costs might be:

Financing launch costs

Public funds: Single Regeneration Budget, New Deal, European Social Fund, TEC and local authority funding, core funding grant	£110,000
Large business donations: sponsorship, secondees, equipment, services in kind	£80,000
Charitable foundations	£10,000
Shortfall to be raised by local fund-raising initiatives	£9,600
Total	**£209,600**

In addition, the EM would need to receive funds from similar sources, or to borrow, to cover any deficit between membership income and running costs in subsequent years, until viability was achieved (see 4 below).

(b) Running costs
We assume the employee mutual will incur these running costs once fully operational (years two and three). We assume an annual inflation rate of 3 per cent.

Running costs

Item	Year Two (£)	Year Three (£)
Staff		
Chief executive	27,810	28,644
Job search/placement coordinator	21,115	21,748
Childcare coordinator	21,115	21,748
Benefits coordinator	21,115	21,748
Self-employed services coordinator	21,115	21,748
Training coordinator	21,115	21,748
Administrative support	14,420	14,852
	147,805	152,236
Plus NI/pensions @ 16%	*171,454*	*176,594*
General costs		
Rent	7,210	7,426
Postage, photocopying, stationery, telephone	7,000	7,210
Travel	1,545	1,591
Equipment, furniture & maintenance	3,000	3,090
Computers & maintenance	5,000	5,150
Financial management, auditing, insurance	10,506	10,821
Sundry	4,120	4,243
Staff training/away days	3,090	3,182
Advertising/marketing	15,000	15,450
Communications/events for members	7,000	7,210
Total general costs	*63,471*	*65,373*
Total costs	**234,925**	**241,967**

4. Financial viability

This analysis of the employee mutual's finances shows that it would be able to cover its basic costs using membership fees. This assumes that the mutual is able to cover its launch costs (plus any deficits during its first couple of years) from public funds, corporate donations and other fundraising. At the lower rate of contributions, the EM would be financially viable in year three, and at the higher rate it would be viable in year two. Any surplus of membership fees over costs could be used by the EM to finance services to its members and/or to invest in trading activities.

Financial summary

	Launch Year One	Year Two	Year Three
Costs (£)	209,600	234,925	241,967
Income (£) from Membership Fees			
@ Higher Rate Contributions	0	241,280	396,240
@ Lower Rate Contributions	0	153,400	249,600

5. Paying for services

The services provided by the employee mutual would be financed in the following ways:

Membership fees

Any surplus membership fees after running costs could be used to help finance services.

Services in kind

We assume that each unemployed member will put into the mutual fifteen hours of work a week (for 48 weeks each year), providing services in kind such as childcare, job search, marketing, administration and maintenance. This work, which would be organised by the full-time coordinators referred to above, would enable the mutual to provide services at reduced cost, or in some cases at no charge. It is difficult to put a monetary value on the services in kind provided by members to one another, but we place a notional value on this work of 65 per cent of the likely national minimum wage of £3.60 per hour. This means the notional value of a week's work for the mutual by an unemployed member would be £35.10. On the basis of the membership projections in the business plan, the value of the services in kind provided by unemployed members would be approximately:

Value of services in kind

Months into Development	Number of Unemployed Members	Notional Annual Income in Kind (£)
0	0	0
6	0	0
12	600	1,010,880
18	840	1,415,232
24	1,040	1,752,192
30	1,080	1,819,584
36	1,100	1,853,280

Additional services in kind would be provided by employed and employer members. Services provided by the former would include mentoring for unemployed members. Contributions from employers, such as secondees, and spare spaces on their in-house training courses, would also help lower the cost of services.

Public funds

The EM would be eligible for public funds, including the Single Regeneration Budget, local authority economic development funds, the New Deal and TEC funding. These funds would typically be granted for specific employment or training programmes run by the EM for its members. Depending on the eligibility criteria for funding, participating members might have to be unemployed or working in small firms.

Charging for services

The EM would charge employee, self-employed and employer members for its services. The charges paid would reflect the mutual's low costs and the other contributions (both membership fees and services in kind) being made by the member, as well as the member's ability to pay. Trade within the mutual might enjoy tax advantages. The EM would also offer some of its services, such as recruitment, training and childcare, to non-members at commercial rates. We do not attempt to estimate the size of this trading income; the likelihood is that it would take some time for a new mutual to establish a reputation in the market.